THE ACT OF UNION OF 1707

Anne Stuart, Queen of Great Britain,
Queen of Ireland

Edited by: D.P. Curtin

Dalcassian
Publishing
Company

The Act of Union of 1707

All rights reserved. No part of the material protected by this copyright may be reproduced or utilized in any form, electronic or mechanical, including photocopying, recording or by any information storage and retrieval system, without written permission from the copyright owner.

Library of Congress Cataloging-in-Publication Data

Copyright © 2018 Dalcassian Publishing Co.
In association with St. Macartan Press
All rights reserved.

The Act of Union of 1707

The Act of Union of 1707

Act ratifying and approving treaty of the two Kingdoms of Scotland and England. [January 16, 1707]

The Estates of Parliament, considering that Articles of Union of the Kingdoms of Scotland and England were agreed on 22nd of July, 1706 by the Commissioners nominated on behalf of this Kingdom, under Her Majesties Great Seal of Scotland bearing date the 27th of February last past, in pursuance of the fourth Act of the third Session of this Parliament and the Commissioners nominated on behalf of the Kingdom of England under Her Majesties Great Seal of England bearing date at Westminster the tenth day of April last past in pursuance of an Act of Parliament made in England the third year of Her Majesties Reign to treat of and concerning an Union of the said Kingdoms Which Articles were in all humility presented to Her Majesty upon the twenty third of the said Month of July and were Recommended to this Parliament by Her Majesties Royal Letter of the date the 31st day of July, 1706; and that the said Estates of Parliament have agreed to, and approve of the said Articles of Union, with some additions.

And that the said Estates of Parliament have agreed to and approve of the said Articles of Union with some Additions and Explanations as is contained in the Articles hereafter insert And sicklyke Her Majesty with advice and consent of the Estates of Parliament Resolving to Establish the Protestant Religion and Presbyterian Church Government within this Kingdom has past in this Session of Parliament an Act entituled Act for secureing of the Protestant Religion and Presbyterian Church Government which by the Tenor thereof is appointed to be insert in any Act ratifying the Treaty and expressly declared to be a fundamentall and essentiall Condition of the said Treaty or Union in all time coming.

Therefore Her Majesty with advice and consent of the Estates of Parliament in fortification of the Approbation of the Articles as above mentioned And for their further and better Establishment of the same upon full and mature deliberation upon the forsaids Articles of Union and Act of Parliament Doth Ratifie Approve and Confirm the same with the Additions and Explanations contained in the saids Articles in manner and under the provision aftermentioned whereof the Tenor follows.

Article 1 (name of the new kingdom)

That the Two Kingdoms of Scotland and England, shall upon the 1st May next ensuing the date hereof, and forever after, be United into One Kingdom by the Name of GREAT BRITAIN: And that the Ensigns Armorial of the said United Kingdom be such as Her Majesty shall think fit, and used in all Flags, Banners, Standards and Ensigns both at Sea and Land.

Article 2 (succession to the throne)

That the Succession to the Monarchy of the United Kingdom of Great Britain and of the Dominions thereunto belonging after Her Most Sacred Majesty, and in default of Issue of Her Majesty be, remain and continue to the Most Excellent Princess Sophia Electoress and Dutchess Dowager of Hanover, and the Heirs of Her body, being Protestants, upon whom the Crown of England is settled by an Act of Parliament made in England in the twelfth year of the Reign of His late Majesty King William the Third entituled An Act for the further Limitation of the Crown and better securing the Rights and Liberties of the Subject;

And that all Papists and persons marrying Papists, shall be excluded from and forever incapable to inherit possess or enjoy the Imperial Crown of Great Britain, and the Dominions thereunto belonging or any part thereof; And in every such case the Crown and Government shall from time to time descend to, and be enjoyed by such person being a Protestant as should have inherited and enjoyed the same, in case such Papists or person marrying a Papist was naturally dead, according to the provision for the Descent of the Crown of England, made by another Act of Parliament in England in the first year of the Reign of their late Majesties King William and Queen Mary entituled an Act declaring the Rights and Liberties of the Subject, and settling the Succession of the Crown.

Article 3 (united parliament)

That the United Kingdom of Great Britain be Represented by one and the same Parliament, to be stiled the Parliament of Great Britain.

Article 4 (equal privileges of subjects)

That the Subjects of the United Kingdom of Great Britain shall from and after the Union have full Freedom and Intercourse of Trade and Navigation to and from any port or place within the said United Kingdom and the Dominions and Plantations thereunto belonging. And that there be a Communication of all other Rights, Privileges and Advantages which do or may belong to the Subjects of either Kingdom except where it is otherwayes expressly agreed in these Articles.

Article 5 (ships)

That all ships or vessels belonging to Her Majesties Subjects of Scotland at the time of Ratifying the Treaty of Union of the Two Kingdoms in the Parliament of Scotland though foreign built be deemed and pass as ships of the build of Great Britain; the Owner or where there are more Owners, one or more of the Owners within Twelve Months after the first of May next making oath that at the time of Ratifying the Treaty of Union in the Parliament of Scotland, the same did in haill or in part belong to him or them, or to some other Subject of Subjects of Scotland, to be particularly named with the place of their respective abodes, and that the same doth then at the time of the said Deposition wholly belong to him or them, and that no forreigner directly or indirectly hath any share part or interest therein, Which Oath shall be made before the chief Officer or Officers of the Customs in the Port next to the abode of the said Owner or Owners;

And the said Officer or Officers shall be Impowered to administer the said Oath, And the Oath being so administred shall be attested by the Officer or Officers who administred the same And being Registred by the said Officer or Officers, shall be delivered to the Master of the ship for security of her Navigation and a Duplicate thereof shall be transmitted by the said Officer or Officers to the Chief Officer or Officers of the Customs in the port of Edinburgh, to be there Entered in a Register and from thence to be sent to the port of London to be there Entered in the General Register of all Trading ships belonging to Great Britain.

Article 6 (customs union)

That all parts of the United Kingdom for ever from and after the Union shall have the same Allowances, Encouragements and Drawbacks, and be under the same Prohibitions, Restrictions and Regulations of Trade and lyable to the same Customs and Duties on Import and Export. And that the Allowances Encouragements and Drawbacks Prohibitions Restrictions and Regulations of Trade and the Customs and Duties on Import and Export settled in England when the Union commences shall from and after the Union take place throughout the whole United Kingdom, excepting and reserving the Duties upon Export and Import of such particular Commodities from which any persons the Subjects of either Kingdom are specially Liberated and Exempted by their private Rights which after the Union are to remain safe and entire to them in all respects as before the same.

And that from and after the Union no Scots Cattle carried into England shall be lyable to any other Duties either on the publick or private Accounts than these Duties to which the Cattle of England are or shall be lyable within the said Kindgom. And seeing by the Laws of England there are Rewards granted upon the Exportation of certain kinds of Grain wherein Oats grinded or ungrinded are not expressed, that from and after the Union when Oats shall be sold at 15 shillings Sterling per quarter of the Oat-meal exported in the terms of the Law whereby and so long as Rewards are granted for Exportation of other Grains. And that the Bear of Scotland have the same Rewards as Barley.

And in respect the Importation of Victual into Scotland from any place beyond Sea would prove a Discouragement to Tillage, Therefore that the Prohibition as now in force by the Law of Scotland against Importation of Victual from Ireland or any other place beyond Sea into Scotland, do after the Union remain in the same force as now it is until more proper and effectuall ways be provided by the Parliament of Great Britain for discouraging the Importation of the said Victual from beyond Sea.

Article 7 (tax on liquor)

That all parts of the United Kingdom be for ever from and after the Union lyable to the same Excises upon all Exciseable Liquors excepting only that the 34 Gallons English Barrel of Beer or Ale amounting to 12 Gallons Scots present measure sold in Scotland by the Brewer at 9/6d Sterling excluding all Duties and Retailed including Duties and the Retailer's profit at 2d the Scots pint or eight part of the Scots Gallon, be not after the Union lyable on account of the present Excise upon Exciseable Liquors in England, to any higher Imposition than 2s Sterling upon the forsaid 34 Gallons English barrel, being 12 gallons the present Scots measure And that the Excise settled in England on all other Liquors when the Union commences take place throughout the whole United Kingdom.

Article 8 (tax on salt, meat and fish)

That from and after the Union all forreign Salt which shall be Imported into Scotland shall be charged at the Importation there with the same Duties as the like Salt is now charged with being Imported into England and to be levied and secured in the same manner. But in regard the Duties of great quantities of forreign Salt Imported may be very heavie on the Merchants Importers; That therefor all forreign Salt imported into Scotland shall be Cellared and Locked up under the custody of the Merchant Importer and the Officers imployed for levying the Duties upon Salt And that the Merchant may have what quantities thereof his occasion may require not under a Weigh or fourtie Bushells at a time; Giving security for the duty of what quantity he receives payable in six Months. But Scotland shall for the space of seven Years from the said Union be Exempted from paying in Scotland for Salt made there the Dutie or Excise now payable for Salt made in England:

But from the Expiration of the said seven years shall be subject and lyable to the same Duties for Salt make in Scotland, as shall be then payable for Salt made in England, to be levied and secured in the same manner and with proportional Drawbacks and Allowances as in England, with this exception that Scotland shall after the said seven years remain exempted from the Duty of 2s 4d a Bushell on home Salt Imposed by ane Act made in England in the Ninth and Tenth of King William the Third of England.

The Act of Union of 1707

And if the Parliament of Great Britain shall at or before the expiring of the said seven years substitute any other fund in place of the said 2s 4d of Excise on the bushel of Home Salt, Scotland shall after the said seven years, bear a proportion of the said Fund, and have an Equivalent in the Terms of this Treaty, And that during the said seven years there shall be payed in England for all Salt made in Scotland and imported from thence into England the same duties upon the Importation as shall be payable for Salt made in England and levied and secured in the same manner as the Duties on forreign Salt are to be levied and secured in England.

And that after the said seven years how long the said Duty of 2s 4d a Bushel upon Salt is continued in England the said 2s 4d a Bushel shall be payable for all Salt made in Scotland and imported into England, to be levied and secured in the same manner And that during the continuance of the Duty of 2s 4d a Bushel upon Salt made in England no Salt whatsoever be brought from Scotland to England by Land in any manner under the penalty of forfeiting the Salt and the Cattle and Carriages made use of in bringing the same and paying 20s for every Bushel of such Salt, and proportionably for a greater or lesser quantity, for which the Carrier as well as the Owner shall be lyable jointly and severally, And the persons bringing or carrying the same, to be imprisoned by any one Justice of the Peace, by the space of six months without Bail, and until the penalty by payed:

And for Establishing an equality Trade That all Fleshes exported from Scotland to England and put on Board in Scotland to be Exported to parts beyond the Seas and provisions for ships in Scotland and for forreign voyages may be salted with Scots Salt paying the same Dutie for what Salt is so employed as the like quantity of such Salt pays in England and under the same penalties forfeitures and provisions for preventing of frauds as are mentioned in the Laws of England And that from and after the Union the Laws and Acts of Parliament in Scotland for Pineing Curing and Packing of Herrings White Fish and Salmond for Exportation with Forreign Salt only without any mixture of British or Irish Salt and for preventing of frauds in Curing and Packing of Fish be continued in force in Scotland subject to such alterations as shall be made by the Parliament of Great Britain.

And that all Fish exported from Scotland to parts beyond the Seas which shall be Cured with Forreign Salt only and without mixture of British or Irish Salt, shall have the same Eases Premiums and Drawbacks as are or shall be allowed to such persons as Export the like Fish from England: And that for Encouragement of the Herring Fishing there shall be allowed and payed to the Subjects Inhabitants of Great Britain during the present allowances for other Fishes 10s 5d Sterling for every Barrel of White Herrings which shall be exported from Scotland; And that there shall be allowed 5s Sterling for every Barrel of Beef of Pork salted with Forreign Salt without mixture of British or Irish Salt and Exported for sale from Scotland to parts beyond Sea alterable by the Parliament of Great Britain.

And if any matters of fraud relating to the said Duties on Salt shall hereafter appear which are not sufficiently provided against by this Article the same shall be subject to such further provisions as shall be thought fit by the Parliament of Great Britain.

Article 9 (proportionate taxation)

That whenever the sum of £1,997,763 8s 4d (and one) half penny shall be Enacted by the Parliament of Great Britain to be raised in that part of the United Kingdom now called England, on Land and other things usually charged in Acts of Parliament there for granting an aid to the Crown by a Land Tax; that part of the United Kingdom now called Scotland shall be charged by the same Act with a further sum of £48,000 free of all Charges, as the Quota of Scotland to such Tax, and so proportionably for any greater or lesser sum raised in England by any Tax on Land and other things usually charged, together with the Land And that such Quota for Scotland in the cases aforesaid, be raised and collected in the same manner as the Cess now is in Scotland, but subject to such Regulations in the manner of Collecting, as shall be made by the Parliament of Great Britain.

Article 10 (English stamp tax not to apply to Scotland)

That during the continuance of the respective Duties on Stampt paper, Vellom and Parchment, by the severall Acts now in force in England, Scotland shall not be charged with the same respective Duties.

Article 11 (English window tax not to apply to Scotland)

That during the continuance of the Duties payable in England on Windows and Lights which determines on 1st August 1710 Scotland shall not be charged with the same Duties.

Article 12 (English coal tax not to apply to Scotland)

That during the continuance of the Duties payable in England on Coals, Culm and Cinders, which determines 30th September 1710 Scotland shall not be charged therewith for Coals Culm and Cinders consumed there but shall be charged with the same Duties as in England for all Coals, Culm and Cinders not consumed in Scotland.

Article 13 (English malt tax not to apply to Scotland)

That during the continuance of the Duty payable in England on Malt, which determines 24th June 1707, Scotland shall not be charged with that Duty.

Article 14 (any other pre-existing English taxes not to apply to Scotland)

That the Kingdom of Scotland be not Charged with any other Duties laid on by the Parliament of England before the Union except these consented to in this Treaty, in regard it is agreed, That all necessary Provision shall be made by the Parliament of Scotland for the publick Charge and Service of that Kingdom for the year 1707: Provided nevertheless That if the Parliament of England shall think fit to lay any further Impositions by way of Customs, or such Excises, with which by virtue of this Treaty, Scotland is to be charged equally with England, in such case Scotland shall be lyable to the same Customs and Excises, and have an Equivalent to be settled by the Parliament of Great Britain;

With this further provision That any Malt to be made and consumed in that part of the United Kingdom now called Scotland shall not be charged with any Imposition upon Malt during this present War;

And seeing that it cannot be supposed that the Parliament of Great Britain will ever lay any sorts of Burthens upon the United Kingdom, but what they shall find necessity at that time for the

Preservation and Good of the whole, and with due regard to the Circumstances and Abilities of every part of the United Kingdom Therefore it is agreed That there be no further Exemption insisted upon for any part of the United Kingdom, but that the consideration of any Exemption beyond that already agreed on in this Treaty, shall be left to the determination of the Parliament of Great Britain.

Article 15 (economics of balancing taxation)

Whereas by the Terms of this Treaty the Subjects of Scotland for preserving an Equality of Trade throughout the United Kingdom, will be lyable to severall Customs and Excises now payable in England, which will be applicable towards payment of the Debts of England, contracted before the Union;

It is agreed, That Scotland shall have an Equivalent for what the Subjects thereof shall be so charged towards payment of the said Debts of England, in all particulars whatsoever, in manner following viz.

That before the Union of the said Kingdoms, the sum of £398,085 10s be granted to Her Majesty by the Parliament of England for the uses aftermentioned, being the Equivalent to be answered to Scotland for such parts of the saids Customs and Excises upon all Exciseable Liquors, with which that Kingdom is to be charged upon the Union, as will be applicable to the payment of the said Debts of England, according to the proportions which the present Customs in Scotland, being £30,000 per annum : And which the present Excises on Excisable Liquors in Scotland, do bear to the Customs in England, computed at &pounds;1,341,559 per annum;

And which the present Excises on Excisable Liquors in Scotland, being £33,500 per annum, do bear to the Excises and Excisable Liquors in England, computed at £947,602 per annum; Which sum of £398,085 10s, shall be due and payable from the time of the Union:

And in regard That after the Union Scotland becoming lyable to the same Customs and Duties payable on Import and Export, and to the same Excises on all Exciseable Liquors as in England as well as upon that account as upon the account of the Increase of Trade and

The Act of Union of 1707

People (which will be the happy consequence of the Union)* the said Revenues will much improve beyond the before mentioned annual values thereof, of which no present Estimate can be made, Yet nevertheless for the reasons aforesaid there ought to be a proportionable Equivalent answered to Scotland It is agreed That after the Union there shall be an Accompt kept of the said Duties arising in Scotland, to the end it may appear, what ought to be answered to Scotland, as an Equivalent for such proportion of the said encrease as shall be applicable to the payment of Debts of England.

And for the further and more effectuall answering the severall ends hereafter mentioned It is agreed that from and after the Union, the whole Encrease of the Revenues of Customs, and Duties on Import and Export, and Excise upon Exciseable Liquors in Scotland over and above the annual produce of the said respective Duties, as above stated, shall go and be applied, for the term of seven years, to the uses hereafter mentioned; And that upon the said account, there shall be answered to Scotland annually from the end of seven years after the Union, an Equivalent in proportion to such part of the said Increase as shall be applicable to the Debts of England, And generally that an Equivalent shall be answered to;

And as for the uses to which the said sum of £398,085 10s to be granted as aforesaid and all other monies, which are to be answered or allowed to Scotland as said is are to be applied It is agreed That in the first place out of the foresaid sum what consideration shall be found necessary to be had for any Losses which privat persons may sustain by reducing the Coin of Scotland to the Standard and Value of the Coin of England may be made good In the next place That the Capital Stock or fund of the African and Indian Company of Scotland advanced together with the interest for the said Capital Stock after the rate of 5% per annum from the respective times of the payment thereof shall be payed; Upon payment of which Capital Stock and Interest It is agreed The said Company be dissolved and cease And also that from the time of passing the Act of Parliament in England for raising the said sum of £398,085 10s the said Company shall neither Trade nor Grant Licence to Trade Providing that if the said Stock and Interest shall not be payed in twelve months after the Commencement of the Union That then the said Company may from thence forward Trade or give Licence to Trade until the said hail Capital Stock and Interest shall be payed:

And as to the Overplus of the said sum of £398,085 10s after payment of what consideration shall be had for losses in repairing the Coin and paying the said Capital Stock and Interest, and also the hail increase of the said Revenues of Customs Duties and Excises above the present value which shall arise in Scotland during the said term of seven years together with the Equivalent which shall become due upon the Improvement thereof in Scotland after the said term and also as to all other sums which according to the agreements aforesaid may become payable to Scotland by way of Equivalent for what that Kingdom shall hereafter become Scotland for such parts of the English Debts as Scotland may hereafter become lyable to pay by reason of the Union, other than such for which appropriations have been made by Parliament in England of the Customs, or other duties on Export and Import Excises on all Exciseable Liquors, in respect of which Debts, Equivalents are herein before provided.

Article 16 (monetary union)

That from and after the Union the Coin shall be of the same standard and value, throughout the United Kingdom, as now in England, And a Mint shall be continued in Scotland under the same Rules as the Mint in England And the present Officers of the Mint continued subject to such Regulations and Alterations as Her Majesty Her Heirs or Successors, or the Parliament of Great Britain shall think fit.

Article 17 (common weights and measures)

That from and after the Union the same Weights and Measures shall be used throughout the United Kingdom as are now Established in England; And Standards of Weights and Measures shall be kept by those Burroughs in Scotland, to whom the keeping the Standards of Weights and Measures now in use there does of speciall Right belong; All which Standards shall be sent down to such respective Burroughs from the Standards kept in the Exchequer at Westminster, subject nevertheless to such Regulations as the Parliament of Great Britain shall think fit.

Article 18 (common trade laws)

That the Laws concerning Regulation of Trade, Customs, and such Excises, to which Scotland is by virtue of this Treaty to be liable, be the same in Scotland, from and after the Union as in England; and that all other Laws, in use within the Kingdom of Scotland do after the Union, and notwithstanding thereof, remain in the same force as before (except such as are contrary to or inconsistent with this Treaty) but alterable by the Parliament of Great Britain, With this difference betwixt the Laws concerning publick right Policy, and Civil Government, and those which concern private right and the Laws which concern publick right Policy and Civil Government may be made the same throughout the whole United Kingdom; but that no alteration be made in Laws which concern private Right, except for the evident utility of the subjects within Scotland.

Article 19 (judiciaries to remain separate)

That the Court of Session or Colledge of Justice, do after the Union and notwithstanding thereof, remain in all time coming within Scotland as it is now constituted by the Laws of that Kingdom, and with the same Authority and Priviledges as before the Union; subject nevertheless to such Regulations for the better Administration of Justice as shall be made by the Parliament of Great Britain; And that hereafter none shall be named by Her Majesty or Her Royal Successors to be Ordinary Lords of Session but such who have served in the Colledge of Justice as Advocats or Principal Clerks of Session for the space of five years, or as Writers to the Signet for the space of ten years With this provision That no Writer to the Signet be capable to be admitted a Lord of the Session unless he undergo a private and publick Tryal on the Civil Law before the Faculty of Advocats and be found by them qualified for the said Office two years before he be named to be a Lord of the Session, yet so as the Qualifications made or to be made for capacitating persons to be named Ordinary Lords of Session may be altered by the Parliament of Great Britain.

And that the Court of Justiciary do also after the Union, and notwithstanding thereof remain in all time coming within Scotland, as it is now constituted by the Laws of that Kingdom, and with the same Authority and Priviledges as before the Union; subject nevertheless to such Regulations as shall be made by the Parliament of Great Britain, and without prejudice of other Rights of Justiciary:

And that all Admiralty Jurisdictions be under the Lord High Admirall or Commissioners for the Admiralty of Great Britain for the time being; And that the Court of Admiralty now Established in Scotland be continued, And that all Reviews, Reductions or Suspensions of the Sentences in Maritime Cases competent to the Jurisdiction of that Court remain the the same manner after the Union as now in Scotland, until the Parliament of Great Britain shall make such Regulations and Alterations, as shall be judged expedient for the whole United Kingdom, so as there be alwayes continued in Scotland a Court of Admiralty such as in England, for determination of all Maritime Cases relating to private Rights in Scotland competent to the Jurisdiction of the Admiralty Court; subject nevertheless to such Regulations and Alterations as shall be thought proper to be made by the Parliament of Great Britain; And that the Heritable Rights of Admiralty and Vice-Admiralties in Scotland be reserved to the respective Proprietors as Rights of Property, subject nevertheless, as to the manner of Exercising such Heritable Rights to such Regualtions and Alterations as shall be thought proper to be made by the Parliament of Great Britain;

And that all other Courts now in being within the Kingdom of Scotland do remain, but subject to Alterations by the Parliament of Great Britain; And that all Inferior Courts within the said Limits do remain subordinate, as they are now to the Supream Courts of Justice within the same in all time coming;

And that no Causes in Scotland be cognoscible by the Courts of Chancery, Queens-Bench, Common-Pleas, or any other Court in Westminster-hall; And that the said Courts, or any other of the like nature after the Union, shall have no power to Cognosce, Review or Alter the Acts or Sentences of the Judicatures within Scotland, or stop the Execution of the same;

And that there be a Court of Exchequer in Scotland after the Union, for deciding Questions concerning the Revenues of Customs and Excises there, having the same power and authority in such cases, as the Court of Exchequer has in England And that the said Court of Exchequer in Scotland have power of passing Signatures, Gifts

Tutories, and in other things as the Court of Exchequer in Scotland hath; And that the Court of Exchequer that now is in Scotland do remain, until a New Court of Exchequer be settled by the Parliament of Great Britain in Scotland after the Union;

And that after the Union the Queens Majesty and Her Royal Successors, may Continue a Privy Council in Scotland, for preserving of public Peace and Order, until the Parliament of Great Britain shall think fit to alter it or establish any other effectual method for that end.

Article 20 (titles, etc., are rights of property)

That all heritable Offices, Superiorities, heritable Jurisdictions, Offices for life, and Jurisdictions for life, be reserved to the Owners thereof, as Rights of Property, in the same manner as they are now enjoyed by the Laws of Scotland, notwithstanding of this Treaty.

Article 21 (rights of Scottish royal boroughs unaffected)

That the Rights and Privileges of the Royall Burroughs in Scotland as they now are, Do Remain entire after the Union, and notwithstanding thereof.

Article 22 (representative peers; definition of terms)

That by virtue of this Treaty, Of the Peers of Scotland at the time of the Union 16 shall be the number to Sit and Vote in the House of Lords, and 45 the number of the Representatives of Scotland in the House of Commons of the Parliament of Great Britain; And that when Her Majesty Her Heirs or Successors, shall Declare Her or their pleasure for holding the first or any subsequent Parliament of Great Britain until the Parliament of Great Britain shall make further provision therein, A Writ do issue under the Great Seal of the United Kingdom, Directed to the Privy Council of Scotland, Commanding them to Cause 16 Peers, who are to sit in the House of Lords to be Summoned to Parliament and 45 Members to be Elected to sit in the House of Commons of the Parliament of Great Britain according to the Agreement in the Treaty, in such manner as by a subsequent Act of this present Session of the Parliament of Scotland shall be settled;

Which Act is hereby Declared to be as valid as if it were a part of and ingrossed in this Treaty:

And that the Names of the Persons so Summoned and Elected, shall be Returned by the Privy Council of Scotland into the Court from whence the said Writ did issue. And that if her Majesty, on or before the 1st day of May next, on which day the Union is to take place shall Declare under the Great Seal of England, That it is expedient, that the Lords of Parliament of England, and Commons of the present Parliament of England should be the Members of the respective Houses of the first Parliament of Great Britain for and on the part of England, then the said Lords of Parliament of England, and Commons of the present Parliament of England, shall be the members of the respective Houses of the first Parliament of Great Britain, for and on the part of England:

And Her Majesty may by Her Royal Proclamation under the Great Seal of Great Britain, appoint the said first Parliament of Great Britain to Meet at such time and place as Her Majesty shall think fit; which time shall not be less than 50 days after the date of such Proclamation; And the time and place of the Meeting of such Parliament being so appointed, a Writ shall be immediately issued under the Great Seal of Great Britain, directed to the Privy Council of Scotland, for the summoning the 16 Peers, and for Electing forty five Members, by whom Scotland is to be Represented in the Parliament of Great Britain:

And the Lords of Parliament of England, and the 16 Peers of Scotland, such 16 Peers being Summoned and Returned in the manner agreed by this Treaty; and the Members of the House of Commons of the said Parliament of England and the 45 Members for Scotland, such 45 Members being Elected and Returned in the manner agreed in this Treaty shall assemble and meet respectively in their respective houses of the Parliament of Great Britain, at such time and place as shall be so appointed by Her Majesty, and shall be the Two houses of the first Parliament of Great Britain, And that Parliament may Continue for such time only as the present Parliament of England might have Continued, if the Union of the Two Kingdoms had not been made, unless sooner Dissolved by Her Majesty;

And that every one of the Lords of Parliament of Great Britain, and every member of the House of Commons of the Parliament of Great Britain in the first and all succeeding Parliaments of Great Britain until the Parliament of Great Britain shall otherwayes Direct, shall take the respective Oaths, appointed to be taken in stead of the Oaths of Allegiance and Supremacy, by an Act of Parliament made in England in the first year of the Reign of the late King William and Queen Mary entituled An Act for the abrogating of the Oaths of Supremacy and Allegiance, and appointing other Oaths, and Make Subscribe and audibly Repeat the Declaration mentioned in an Act of Parliament made in England in the 30th year of the Reign of King Charles the Second entituled An Act for the more effectual preserving the Kings Person and Government by Disabling Papists from sitting in either House of Parliament, and shall take and subscribe the Oath mentioned in An Act of Parliament made in England, in the first year of Her Majesties Reign entituled An Act to Declare the Alterations in the Oath appointed to be taken by the Act Entituled An Act for the further security of His Majesties Person, and the Succession of the Crown in the Protestant Line, and for Extinguishing the Hopes of the pretended Prince of Wales, and all other pretenders and their open and secret Abettors, and for Declaring the Association to be determined, at such time, and in such manner as the Members of both Houses of Parliament of England are by the said respective Acts, directed to take, make and subscribe the same upon the penalties and disabilities in the said respective Acts contained.

And it is Declared and Agreed That these words This Realm, the Crown of this Realm, and the Queen of this Realm, mentioned in the Oaths and Declaration contained in the aforsaid Acts, which were intended to signify the Crown and Realm of England, shall be understood of the Crown and Realm of Great Britain, And that in that sense, the said Oaths and Declaration be taken and subscribed by the members of both Houses of the Parliament of Great Britain.

Article 23 (equal rights of Scottish and English lords)

That the foresaid 16 Peers of Scotland, mentioned in the last preceding Article, to sit in the House of Lords of the Parliament of Great Britain shall have all Priviledges of Parliament which the Peers of England now have, and which They or any Peers of Great

Britain shall have after the Union, and particularly the Right of sitting upon the tryals of Peers: And in case of the tryal of any Peer in time of Adjournment or Prorogation of Parliament, the said 16 Peers shall be summoned in the same manner, and have the same powers and priviledges at such tryal, as any other Peers of Great Britain; And that in case any tryals of Peers shall hereafter happen when there is no Parliament in being, the 16 Peers of Scotland who sate in the last preceeding Parliament, shall be summoned in the same manner and have the same powers and privileges at such tryals as any other Peers of Great Britain;

And that all Peers of Scotland, and their successors to their Honours and Dignities, shall from and after the Union be Peers of Great Britain, and have Rank and Precedency next and immediately after the Peers of the like orders and degrees in England at the time of the Union, and before all Peers of Great Britain of the like orders and degrees, who may be Created after the Union, and shall be tryed as Peers of Great Britain, and shall Enjoy all Privileges of Peers, as fully as the Peers of England do now, or as they, or any other Peers of Great Britain may hereafter Enjoy the same except the Right and Privilege of sitting in the House of Lords and the Privileges depending thereon, and particularly the Right of sitting upon the tryals of Peers.

Article 24 (the Great Seal, lesser seals and the Scottish crown jewels)

That from and after the Union, there be One Great Seal for the United Kingdom of Great Britain, which shall be different from the Great Seal now used in either Kingdom; And that the Quartering the Arms and the Rank and Precedency of the Lyon King of Arms of the Kingdom of Scotland as may best suit the Union be left to Her Majesty: And that in the mean time the Great Seal of England be used as the Great Seal of the United Kingdom, and that the Great Seal of the United Kingdom be used for Sealing Writs to Elect and Summon the Parliament of Great Britain and for sealing all Treaties with Forreign Princes and States, and all publick Acts Instruments and Orders of State which Concern the whole United Kingdom, and in all other matters relating to England, as the Great Seal of England is now used, and that a Seal in Scotland after the Union be always kept and made use of in all things relating to private Rights or

Grants, which have usually passed the Great Seal of Scotland, and which only concern Offices, Grants, Commissions, and private Rights within the Kingdom, And that until such Seal shall be appointed by Her Majesty the present Great Seal of Scotland shall be used for such purposes;

And that the Privy Seal, Signet, Casset, Signet of the Justiciary Court, Quarter Seal, and Seals of Courts now used in Scotland be Continued, but that the said Seals be altered and adapted to the state of the Union as Her Majesty shall think fit; And the said Seals, and all of them, and the Keepers of them, shall be subject to Regulations as the Parliament of Great Britain shall hereafter make:

And that the Crown, Scepter and Sword of State, the Records of Parliament, and all other Records, Rolls and Registers whatsoever, both publick and private generall and particular, and Warrands thereof Continue to be keeped as they are within that part of the United Kingdom now called Scotland, and that they shall so remain in all time coming, notwithstanding of the Union.

Article 25 (repeal of conflicting laws)

That all Laws and Statutes in either Kingdom so far as they are contrary to, or inconsistent with the Terms of these Articles, or any of them, shall from and after the Union cease and become void, and shall be so declared to be by the respective Parliaments of the said Kingdoms.

The Act of Union of 1707

The Act of Union of 1707

www.ingramcontent.com/pod-product-compliance
Lightning Source LLC
LaVergne TN
LVHW021750060526
838200LV00052B/3570